Shodan from Zero to Hero

The Ultimate Guide to Cybersecurity & Network Intelligence

Chapter 1: Introduction to Shodan

What is Shodan?

S hodan is often referred to as "the search engine for the Internet of Things (IoT)," but its capabilities go far beyond that. Unlike traditional search engines like Google or Bing, which index web pages, Shodan indexes devices and services connected to the internet. This includes routers, security cameras, industrial control systems (ICS), servers, databases, and much more.

Shodan continuously scans the internet for publicly accessible devices and collects metadata about them, such as IP addresses, open ports, services running on those ports, SSL certificates, and banners that reveal software versions. It is an invaluable tool for cybersecurity professionals, researchers, and IT administrators looking to understand the exposure of their networks and improve security.

How Shodan Differs from Google and Other Search Engines

While Google, Bing, and other traditional search engines focus on indexing and retrieving web content, Shodan operates on a completely different level by scanning the internet for connected devices. Below are some key differences:

1. **Indexing Scope:**
   - Google indexes web pages, text, and multimedia content.
   - Shodan indexes internet-connected devices, services, and their metadata.
2. **Search Queries:**
   - Google searches for keywords and phrases in web pages.
   - Shodan searches for specific IP addresses, open ports, device types, and software versions.
3. **Purpose and Use Case:**
   - Google is primarily used for retrieving information from websites.
   - Shodan is used for cybersecurity research, penetration testing, network monitoring, and vulnerability assessment.
4. **Real-Time Exposure:**

- Google shows content based on previously crawled web pages.
- Shodan provides real-time insights into internet-exposed systems.

Because of these differences, Shodan is widely used by security professionals to detect vulnerable systems before attackers exploit them.

Ethical Considerations and Responsible Usage

Due to the powerful nature of Shodan, it is essential to use it responsibly and ethically. Misusing Shodan for unauthorized access, hacking, or cyberattacks is illegal and unethical. Below are some key guidelines for responsible usage:

1. **Legal Compliance:** Always adhere to local and international laws regarding cybersecurity and unauthorized access.
2. **Permission-Based Testing:** If using Shodan for security assessments, ensure you have explicit permission from the network owner.
3. **Reporting Vulnerabilities:** If you discover an exposed system with potential security risks, consider notifying the owner or relevant authorities rather than exploiting the vulnerability.

4. **Avoid Malicious Intent:** Never use Shodan for activities such as hacking, unauthorized surveillance, or launching cyberattacks.
5. **Educational and Research Purposes:** Shodan is a powerful tool for learning about network security, improving defenses, and raising awareness about potential threats.

Ethical hackers, cybersecurity researchers, and IT administrators can leverage Shodan to identify vulnerabilities and secure their systems against potential threats.

Setting Up a Shodan Account and API Key

To fully utilize Shodan's capabilities, you need to create an account and obtain an API key. Follow these steps to get started:

1. Creating a Shodan Account

1. Go to the official Shodan website: https://www.shodan.io
2. Click on **Sign Up** in the top-right corner.
3. Enter your **email address**, **username**, and **password** to create an account.
4. Verify your email address by clicking on the confirmation link sent to your inbox.

2. Accessing Your Shodan API Key

Once your account is set up:

1. Log in to your Shodan account.
2. Navigate to **My Account** (accessible from the dropdown menu in the top-right corner).
3. Scroll down to find your **API Key**.
4. Copy and store the API Key securely, as it will be used for advanced queries and integrations with other tools.

3. Understanding API Limits

Shodan offers different account tiers, each with specific API usage limits:

- **Free Account:** Limited searches per month with basic access.
- **Shodan Membership ($49 one-time fee):** Higher limits, API access, and additional features.
- **Shodan API Subscription:** For businesses and professionals needing large-scale access.

Using the API key, you can automate searches, integrate Shodan with security tools, and perform deep analysis of internet-exposed assets.

This chapter provides a solid foundation for understanding Shodan, its differences from traditional search engines, ethical considerations, and how to set up an account. In the next chapter, we will explore the core functionalities of Shodan and how to perform effective searches to gather cybersecurity intelligence.

Chapter 2: Understanding Shodan's Capabilities

How Shodan Scans the Internet

Shodan is often referred to as the "search engine for the Internet of Things (IoT)," but how does it actually work? Unlike traditional search engines like Google or Bing, which index websites, Shodan scans the entire internet for exposed devices, services, and network ports.

Shodan's Scanning Process

1. **IP Range Scanning** – Shodan continuously scans public IP addresses across the internet.
2. **Port Scanning** – It checks for open ports (e.g., 22 for SSH, 80 for HTTP, 443 for HTTPS, 3389 for RDP) to identify accessible services.
3. **Banner Grabbing** – When a port is open, Shodan retrieves metadata (banners) that reveal software versions, configurations, and potential vulnerabilities.
4. **Indexing & Categorization** – Shodan stores this information in its database, making it searchable by users.

Shodan's scanning is automated and persistent, meaning new data is constantly being collected and updated. Unlike Nmap, which requires manual execution, Shodan provides an ongoing and historical view of the internet's exposed assets.

What Kind of Devices and Services Shodan Indexes?

Shodan indexes a wide range of internet-connected devices and services, including but not limited to:

1. Industrial Control Systems (ICS)

- SCADA systems
- Programmable Logic Controllers (PLCs)
- Power grids, water treatment plants, and factories

2. Internet of Things (IoT) Devices

- Smart home systems (cameras, thermostats, lighting)
- Connected cars and industrial IoT sensors
- Medical devices and hospital equipment

3. Network Infrastructure

- Firewalls, routers, and VPNs
- Publicly exposed databases (MongoDB, Elasticsearch, MySQL)
- Remote desktop and SSH servers

4. Web and Cloud Services

- Apache, Nginx, and IIS web servers
- FTP, Telnet, and SMB services
- Misconfigured Amazon S3 buckets and cloud storage

Shodan's ability to expose insecure devices highlights the importance of proper security configurations.

Key Use Cases: Cybersecurity, Penetration Testing, Research, and IoT Security

1. Cybersecurity Monitoring

- Security professionals use Shodan to detect **exposed systems** and prevent data leaks.
- Organizations can proactively monitor their **own networks** for misconfigurations.

2. Penetration Testing & Ethical Hacking

- Ethical hackers leverage Shodan to identify vulnerable services before running exploit attempts.
- Shodan provides insights into **outdated software versions** and known CVEs (Common Vulnerabilities and Exposures).

3. Academic and Threat Research

- Researchers analyze global security trends and **track cyber threats** using Shodan data.
- Reports on **ransomware attacks, botnets, and APT (Advanced Persistent Threat) groups** often use Shodan for intelligence gathering.

4. IoT Security Audits

- IoT devices are frequently **misconfigured** and lack basic security (e.g., default passwords).
- Security teams use Shodan to **identify and secure** exposed smart devices.

Final Thoughts

Shodan is a powerful tool that reveals **the hidden side of the internet**. Understanding its capabilities allows cybersecurity professionals, ethical hackers, and researchers to identify risks, secure networks, and stay ahead of threats.

Chapter 3: Getting Started with Shodan Search

Basic Search Queries

Shodan's search functionality is similar to traditional search engines, but instead of web pages, it indexes internet-connected devices. To begin a search, you can enter general terms in the search bar. Here are some basic examples:

- `apache` – Finds devices running Apache web server.
- `cisco` – Lists Cisco networking devices.
- `default password` – Searches for devices that might have default credentials.
- `webcam` – Shows various internet-connected cameras.

Understanding how to refine searches will help you get more relevant results.

Filtering Results

Shodan allows the use of filters to narrow down search results effectively. Here are some of the most useful filters:

- **`country:`** – Filters results by country. Example: `apache country:US`

- `port:` – Finds devices running on a specific port. Example: `port:22` for SSH servers.
- `org:` – Searches for devices belonging to a specific organization. Example: `org:"Google"`
- `after:` – Finds results indexed after a specific date. Example: `after:2024-01-01`
- `before:` – Searches for devices indexed before a certain date.
- `city:` – Filters results by city. Example: `city:"New York"`
- `product:` – Searches for a specific software or service. Example: `product:nginx`
- `os:` – Looks for a particular operating system. Example: `os:windows`

By combining these filters, you can conduct highly targeted searches. For instance:

```
nginx country:DE port:80 org:"Deutsche Telekom"
```

This search finds Nginx web servers running in Germany on port 80 that belong to Deutsche Telekom.

Understanding Shodan Search Results

When you perform a search, Shodan provides various details about the discovered devices. Understanding these results is crucial:

- **IP Address** – The unique address of the device on the internet.
- **Ports** – Open ports on the device, indicating which services are running.
- **Banners** – Information returned by the service running on a particular port. It often contains version details and configurations.
- **Vulnerabilities** – If Shodan detects known security vulnerabilities, it will display CVE (Common Vulnerabilities and Exposures) identifiers.
- **Location** – Information about where the device is located, including country, city, and sometimes ISP.

For example, a Shodan result may look like this:

```
IP: 203.0.113.45
Port: 22 (SSH)
Banner: OpenSSH 8.0 (protocol 2.0)
Vulnerabilities: CVE-2022-2068, CVE-2019-6111
Location: United States, California
Organization: Cloudflare
```

Finding Open Databases, Webcams, and Industrial Control Systems (ICS)

Shodan is widely used to find exposed systems that should not be publicly accessible. Here are a few key searches to discover such systems:

Open Databases

Exposed databases are a major security risk. You can find them with:

- `product:mongodb` – Searches for open MongoDB instances.
- `port:3306 product:mysql` – Finds MySQL databases.
- `port:5432 product:postgresql` – Searches for PostgreSQL databases.

Webcams

Internet-connected cameras often lack proper security. To find them:

- `port:554 has_screenshot:true` – Finds RTSP (Real-Time Streaming Protocol) cameras.
- `product:"GoAhead"` – Searches for webcams using the GoAhead web server.
- `title:"webcam"` – Looks for web pages with "webcam" in the title.

Industrial Control Systems (ICS)

Many ICS devices should not be publicly exposed, but Shodan can find them:

- `port:502` – Modbus devices.
- `port:44818` – Rockwell Automation devices.

- `port:1911 product:Niagara` — **Tridium Niagara** systems.

Ethical Considerations

Using Shodan comes with responsibility. Unauthorized access to devices is illegal. Always ensure that you have permission to analyze systems, and use Shodan ethically for research, security analysis, and education.

Chapter 4: Advanced Shodan Query Techniques

Shodan is a powerful tool, but to unlock its full potential, you need to master advanced search techniques. In this chapter, we will explore **Boolean operators, filtering strategies, vulnerability searches, and monitoring specific devices and networks**.

Using Boolean Operators (AND, OR, NOT)

Shodan supports **Boolean operators** to refine and customize searches. These operators allow you to include, exclude, or combine multiple search terms.

1. AND Operator

- **Usage:** Finds results containing **all** specified keywords.
- **Example:**

```
nginx

apache AND port:80
```

Finds web servers running Apache on port 80.

2. OR Operator

- **Usage:** Finds results containing **at least one** of the specified terms.
- **Example:**

```
nginx

apache OR nginx
```

Finds web servers running either Apache or Nginx.

3. NOT Operator

- **Usage:** Excludes specific terms from results.
- **Example:**

```
nginx

apache NOT country:US
```

Finds Apache servers but excludes those in the United States.

Using **Boolean operators effectively** helps narrow down results and remove irrelevant data.

Combining Multiple Filters for Precise Searches

Shodan provides **filters** that allow for extremely specific searches. You can combine multiple filters to pinpoint devices with exact characteristics.

Commonly Used Filters:

Filter	Description	Example
country	Search by country	country:DE (Germany)
city	Search by city	city:London
org	Search by organization	org:Google
port	Search by port number	port:22 (SSH)
hostname	Search by domain	hostname:example.com
before / after	Search by date	before:2024-01-01
os	Search by operating system	os:Windows
product	Search by software	product:MySQL

Examples of Advanced Filter Combinations

1. **Find all MySQL databases in the U.S. on port 3306:**

   makefile

   ```
   product:MySQL port:3306 country:US
   ```

2. **Find Cisco routers running outdated firmware:**

   lua

   ```
   product:Cisco os:"IOS 12" -os:"IOS 15"
   ```

3. **Find open Remote Desktop (RDP) servers in Germany:**

   makefile

17

```
port:3389 country:DE
```

By combining filters, you can precisely **target devices, vulnerabilities, and misconfigured systems**.

Searching by Vulnerabilities (CVE IDs)

One of Shodan's most powerful features is its ability to search for devices with **known vulnerabilities (CVEs)**.

How to Search for Vulnerabilities

- Shodan tags devices with known vulnerabilities using **CVE IDs** (Common Vulnerabilities and Exposures).
- The format for searching CVEs is:

```makefile
vuln:CVE-YYYY-NNNN
```

Examples:

1. **Find devices vulnerable to EternalBlue (CVE-2017-0144):**

```makefile
vuln:CVE-2017-0144
```

2. **Find all devices with Log4Shell vulnerability (CVE-2021-44228):**

```makefile
vuln:CVE-2021-44228
```

3. **Find exposed Microsoft Exchange servers with a critical CVE:**

```vbnet
product:"Microsoft Exchange" vuln:CVE-2021-26855
```

By searching for CVE IDs, you can proactively **identify and mitigate security risks** before they are exploited.

Monitoring Specific Devices and Networks

Shodan allows you to **monitor and receive alerts** for specific IPs, devices, or networks.

Setting Up Network Monitoring

- **Monitor an IP range:**

```makefile
net:192.168.1.0/24
```

Finds all devices within a subnet.

- **Monitor a specific organization's assets:**

```
vbnet

org:"Amazon"
```

Lists exposed services belonging to Amazon.

- **Track changes for a particular device:**
  1. Create a **Shodan account**
  2. Go to the **Monitor** section
  3. Set up **IP alerts** for critical systems

Shodan's monitoring tools help **security teams track infrastructure changes and detect new threats in real time**.

Final Thoughts

Mastering advanced Shodan queries gives you **precise control** over your searches, allowing you to find critical security flaws, monitor networks, and gather intelligence efficiently.

Chapter 5: Shodan API for Automation

Introduction to the Shodan API

Shodan is a powerful search engine for discovering devices connected to the internet, and its API provides a programmatic way to interact with its vast database. With the Shodan API, you can automate searches, gather intelligence, monitor devices, and build security tools efficiently. This chapter will guide you through setting up the API, making requests, and leveraging Python to automate tasks.

Setting up the API Key and Making Requests

To use the Shodan API, you need an API key, which you can obtain by following these steps:

1. **Create an account on Shodan** – Go to https://www.shodan.io and sign up.
2. **Retrieve your API key** – Once logged in, navigate to the "API Key" section in your account settings.
3. **Install the Shodan Python module** – Open your terminal or command prompt and run:
4. `pip install shodan`
5. **Set up authentication in Python** – Use the API key to initialize Shodan in your Python scripts:

```
6. import shodan
7.
8. API_KEY = "your_api_key_here"
9. api = shodan.Shodan(API_KEY)
```

Once you have the API key set up, you can start making requests to Shodan's API. For example, to perform a basic search for open RDP (Remote Desktop Protocol) servers, use the following script:

```
try:
    results = api.search("port:3389")
    for result in results['matches']:
        print(f"IP:           {result['ip_str']},
Organization: {result.get('org', 'N/A')}")
except shodan.APIError as e:
    print(f"Error: {e}")
```

Automating Searches with Python

With the API, you can automate security research and reconnaissance. For example, you might want to monitor IoT devices or track vulnerabilities over time. Below is a Python script that searches for devices running outdated versions of OpenSSH:

```
query = "product:OpenSSH"

try:
    results = api.search(query)
    print(f"Found {results['total']} results")
    for result in results['matches']:
        print(f"IP:  {result['ip_str']}   |   OS:
{result.get('os', 'Unknown')}")
except shodan.APIError as e:
    print(f"Error: {e}")
```

To further enhance automation, you can integrate the results into a database or set up email alerts when specific threats are detected.

Building Custom Tools Using Shodan Data

The Shodan API allows you to build custom tools for cybersecurity research, network monitoring, and vulnerability assessment. Below are some practical applications:

1. **Network Exposure Analysis** – Identify open ports and exposed services across your organization.
2. **Automated Threat Intelligence** – Track devices with known vulnerabilities and generate reports.
3. **Monitoring IoT Devices** – Detect insecure webcams, routers, and smart home devices.
4. **Custom Dashboard Development** – Use Shodan data to visualize real-time cybersecurity insights.

Here's a simple script to monitor a list of IP addresses for exposed services:

```
ip_list = ["8.8.8.8", "1.1.1.1"]   # Replace with
actual IPs

for ip in ip_list:
    try:
        host_info = api.host(ip)
        print(f"IP:     {ip},     Open     Ports:
{host_info['ports']}")
    except shodan.APIError as e:
```

```
        print(f"Error  fetching  data  for  {ip}:
{e}")
```

By leveraging the Shodan API, you can create highly efficient security automation tools, providing invaluable insights for cybersecurity professionals and researchers.

Chapter 6: Cybersecurity and Ethical Hacking with Shodan

Shodan is a **powerful tool for cybersecurity professionals and ethical hackers**, providing visibility into **exposed devices, misconfigured services, and security vulnerabilities**. In this chapter, we will explore how Shodan can be used to:

- Identify **exposed and misconfigured devices**
- Detect **IoT security risks** in CCTV, smart homes, and industrial systems
- Find **open ports and vulnerabilities**
- Conduct **responsible security research**

1. Identifying Exposed Devices and Misconfigured Services

Many organizations unknowingly expose **sensitive services** to the internet due to misconfigurations, outdated security policies, or human error. Shodan allows ethical hackers and security professionals to **detect these issues before malicious actors do**.

Commonly Exposed Devices and Services

Device/Service	Risk
Remote Desktop (RDP) (port 3389)	Brute-force attacks, ransomware
SSH Servers (port 22)	Unauthorized access, credential theft
FTP Servers (port 21, 990)	Data leaks, insecure authentication
Databases (MongoDB, MySQL, Elasticsearch, Redis)	Exposed sensitive data, unauthorized access
Unsecured Webcams (CCTV, IP cameras)	Privacy invasion, surveillance risks
SCADA/Industrial Control Systems	Critical infrastructure attacks

Example: Finding Open Remote Desktop (RDP) Servers

Many **brute-force attacks** target exposed **RDP servers**. You can find them using:

```makefile
port:3389
```

To narrow it down further to a specific country:

```makefile
port:3389 country:US
```

To target a specific organization:

```vbnet
port:3389 org:"Microsoft"
```

Example: Detecting Exposed Databases

```vbnet
product:"MongoDB" port:27017
```

This query finds publicly accessible **MongoDB** instances, which are often misconfigured without authentication.

---

2. Detecting IoT Security Risks (CCTV, Smart Homes, Industrial Systems)

IoT Devices Are a Security Nightmare

Internet of Things (IoT) devices are often **insecure by default**, with **default passwords, weak encryption, and poor firmware updates**.

Common IoT Risks Found via Shodan

- **CCTV/IP Cameras** → Can be hacked for surveillance or botnets
- **Smart Homes (Thermostats, Door Locks, Smart TVs)** → Prone to unauthorized access
- **Industrial IoT (SCADA, PLCs)** → Critical infrastructure exposed to attacks

Example: Finding Exposed CCTV Cameras

```vbnet
port:554 "webcamXP"
```

This query finds **publicly accessible cameras** running **webcamXP software**.

Example: Finding Vulnerable Smart Home Devices

```vbnet
port:80 product:"Ubiquiti" country:US
```

This finds **Ubiquiti smart home devices** with open HTTP access.

Real-World Example: The Mirai Botnet Attack

In 2016, the **Mirai malware** infected IoT devices (DVRs, cameras, routers), using their **default passwords** to create a **botnet** that launched one of the **largest DDoS attacks in history**. Shodan is often used to track such vulnerable IoT devices.

---

3. Finding Open Ports and Security Vulnerabilities

Shodan provides **real-time insights** into **open ports** and **vulnerable services**.

How Attackers Exploit Open Ports

- **Port 21 (FTP)** – Often exposed without authentication
- **Port 23 (Telnet)** – Unencrypted remote login, prone to brute-force attacks
- **Port 3306 (MySQL)** – Exposed databases, potential data leaks
- **Port 6379 (Redis)** – Can be exploited for **unauthorized command execution**

Example: Finding Open Telnet Ports

```makefile
port:23
```

This finds **devices running Telnet,** which is a huge security risk.

Example: Finding Devices with Known Vulnerabilities (CVE)

Shodan tags devices with **Common Vulnerabilities and Exposures (CVE IDs).**

```makefile
vuln:CVE-2017-0144
```

This searches for **EternalBlue**, the exploit used in **WannaCry ransomware attacks**.

4. Conducting Responsible Security Research

Shodan is a **double-edged sword**—while it helps **ethical hackers** and **security teams**, it can also be used by **malicious actors**.

Ethical Guidelines for Using Shodan

✓ **Obtain Permission** – Do not scan or test devices without explicit consent.
✓ **Report Security Flaws Responsibly** – If you find an exposed system, notify the owner.
✓ **Follow Legal Regulations** – Unauthorized access to systems is illegal.

How to Report a Security Vulnerability

1. **Identify the organization responsible** for the exposed system.
2. **Use official contact channels** (security@domain.com is often a standard).
3. **Provide a responsible disclosure report**, explaining the risk.
4. **Do not exploit or publicly disclose** vulnerabilities before giving the owner time to fix them.

Final Thoughts

Shodan is a **powerful tool for cybersecurity professionals**, but **ethical use is critical**. By understanding how to **identify exposed systems, detect IoT security flaws, and analyze open ports and vulnerabilities**, ethical hackers can **help protect networks and devices from real-world threats**.

Chapter 7: Shodan for Network Security Professionals

Using Shodan for Attack Surface Analysis

Attack surface analysis is a critical aspect of network security. It involves identifying all publicly accessible assets and understanding their exposure to potential threats. Shodan provides a powerful way to map an organization's attack surface by:

- Identifying exposed services and devices.
- Detecting outdated or vulnerable software versions.
- Mapping open ports and protocols used by publicly accessible systems.
- Discovering misconfigurations that could lead to data breaches.

Practical Example:

To perform an attack surface analysis, use the following Shodan query:

```
org:"Your Organization Name" country:"US"
```

This will return all publicly available assets belonging to your organization in the United States.

By analyzing the results, security teams can prioritize remediation efforts and reduce the risk of unauthorized access.

Monitoring Corporate Assets for Vulnerabilities

Continuous monitoring of corporate assets ensures that new vulnerabilities are detected as soon as they appear. Shodan allows security professionals to:

- Track changes in externally visible infrastructure.
- Detect newly exposed services or devices.
- Identify unauthorized deployments that may introduce security risks.

Setting Up Asset Monitoring:

Use Shodan Monitor to receive alerts whenever new assets are detected or changes occur:

1. Sign up for Shodan Monitor.
2. Add your organization's IP ranges.
3. Configure alerts for specific services or vulnerabilities.

This proactive approach helps mitigate threats before they are exploited by attackers.

Threat Intelligence and Incident Response

Shodan serves as a valuable tool for gathering threat intelligence and responding to security incidents. By analyzing data from Shodan, security teams can:

- Identify active threat actors scanning or exploiting vulnerabilities.
- Investigate compromised assets by looking for unexpected changes.
- Cross-reference security incidents with real-time Shodan data.

Example Use Case:

If an intrusion is detected on a specific server, security analysts can use Shodan to determine if that server was previously exposed with a known vulnerability:

```
ip:xxx.xxx.xxx.xxx
```

This can reveal if the asset was indexed by Shodan before the attack, providing insights into how the breach occurred.

Automating Alerts for Exposed Devices

Automation is key to scaling network security operations. Shodan provides APIs and integrations that enable automated alerts for exposed devices and vulnerabilities.

Steps to Automate Alerts:

1. **Use Shodan Monitor**: Set up alerts for changes in your network.
2. **Integrate with SIEM Solutions**: Connect Shodan to your Security Information and Event Management (SIEM) system.
3. **Write a Python Script**: Use the Shodan API to automatically check for exposed devices and notify security teams.

Example Python script for monitoring an organization's assets:

```
import shodan

API_KEY = "your_api_key_here"
api = shodan.Shodan(API_KEY)

try:
    results = api.search("org:\"Your Organization
Name\"")
    for result in results['matches']:
        print(f"IP: {result['ip_str']} | Port:
{result['port']} | {result['data']}")
except shodan.APIError as e:
    print(f"Error: {e}")
```

This script fetches information about exposed assets related to your organization, helping to streamline security operations.

Conclusion

Shodan is a powerful tool for network security professionals, providing essential capabilities for attack surface analysis, vulnerability monitoring, threat intelligence, and automation. By leveraging Shodan's features, security teams can proactively protect corporate assets and respond to emerging threats more effectively.

Chapter 8: Real-World Case Studies & Examples

Shodan has played a **critical role** in both **cyberattacks** and **cybersecurity defense**. In this chapter, we'll explore:

- **How hackers exploit unsecured devices**
- **How cybersecurity researchers use Shodan for ethical hacking**
- **How businesses protect their networks using Shodan**

---

1. How Hackers Exploit Unsecured Devices

Case Study: The Mirai Botnet (2016) – IoT Devices Turned Into a Cyber Weapon

What Happened?

In 2016, the **Mirai malware** scanned the internet for **IoT devices with default passwords** and took control of them. This created a **massive botnet** that launched one of the **largest DDoS attacks in history**, bringing down sites like **Twitter, Reddit, and Netflix**.

How Hackers Used Shodan

Hackers used **Shodan to find vulnerable IoT devices**, such as:

- **CCTV cameras**
- **Routers**
- **Smart TVs and home automation systems**

Example Shodan Search Used by Hackers

```makefile
port:23 country:US
```

This finds devices running **Telnet**, a highly insecure remote access protocol. Many of these devices still use **default passwords**, making them easy to hijack.

Lesson Learned

◈ **Change default passwords** on all IoT devices.
◈ **Disable unnecessary ports** (Telnet, FTP, etc.).
◈ **Use network monitoring tools** to detect unusual activity.

Case Study: Exposed Industrial Control Systems (SCADA Attack)

What Happened?

Researchers found that **thousands of industrial control systems (SCADA/ICS)** were exposed on the internet due to misconfigurations. Hackers could manipulate **power grids, water treatment plants, and factory automation**.

How Hackers Used Shodan

They searched for industrial control systems using:

```
arduino

"SCADA" "Siemens" country:DE
```

This revealed **German industrial systems** running exposed **Siemens PLCs** (programmable logic controllers).

Potential Consequences

✹ **Power outages** due to hacked energy grids
✹ **Water contamination** due to manipulated treatment plants
✹ **Factory shutdowns** due to altered automation processes

Lesson Learned

♦ **SCADA systems should never be exposed to the public   internet.**
♦ **Use VPNs and strong authentication for remote access.**
♦ **Regularly audit networks using tools like Shodan.**

2. How Cybersecurity Researchers Use Shodan for Ethical Hacking

Case Study: Discovering Exposed Voting Machines

What Happened?

Before the 2020 U.S. elections, security researchers found **over 30,000 internet-connected voting machines** that were **not properly secured**. This posed a **huge risk of tampering**.

How Researchers Used Shodan

They searched for exposed election systems with:

```vbnet
port:3389 "voting machine"
```

This revealed devices running **Remote Desktop Protocol (RDP)**, which is vulnerable to **brute-force attacks**.

Outcome

⬥ **Election security teams were notified** to secure the systems.
⬥ **Firewalls were updated** to block unauthorized RDP access.

Lesson Learned

- ◆ Critical infrastructure should not be directly connected to the internet.
- ◆ Regular cybersecurity audits using Shodan are essential.

Case Study: Finding Unsecured Databases with Millions of Records

What Happened?

A security researcher found **an exposed Elasticsearch database** containing **2 billion records** of personal data, including **names, addresses, phone numbers, and emails**.

How Researchers Used Shodan

They searched for publicly accessible databases using:

```vbnet
product:"Elasticsearch" port:9200
```

This revealed **hundreds of databases** that were **exposed without passwords**.

Outcome

♦ **Companies were alerted** and secured their databases.
♦ **Millions of records were protected from data breaches**.

Lesson Learned

♦ **Databases should always require authentication**.
♦ **Use firewalls to restrict database access**.

3. How Businesses Protect Their Networks Using Shodan

Case Study: A Company Prevents a Data Breach Using Shodan Monitoring

What Happened?

A **financial services company** set up **Shodan monitoring** to **track their public-facing assets**. They discovered:

- **Exposed RDP servers**
- **A misconfigured S3 bucket with sensitive files**

How They Used Shodan

They set up alerts using:

```vbnet
org:"Company Name"
```

This **automatically notified** them when new **exposed assets** appeared.

Outcome

⬥ **They secured their RDP servers** before attackers could exploit them.
⬥ **They fixed their S3 permissions**, preventing a **massive data breach**.

Lesson Learned

⬥ **Companies should monitor their attack surface regularly**.
⬥ **Automating security alerts with Shodan helps prevent breaches**.

Final Thoughts

Shodan can be used for **good or bad**—it's a tool that **ethical hackers, cybersecurity researchers, and businesses** can use to **detect security risks before they become catastrophic**.

⬥ **Hackers exploit unsecured devices** to launch **DDoS attacks, steal data, and sabotage infrastructure**.
⬥ **Cybersecurity researchers use Shodan to identify and report vulnerabilities**.
⬥ **Businesses use Shodan to proactively secure their networks**.

Chapter 9: Best Practices & Legal Considerations

Ethical Hacking Guidelines

When using Shodan, it is crucial to follow ethical hacking principles. Ethical hacking involves exploring systems and networks to identify vulnerabilities with permission and good intent. Here are key ethical guidelines to follow:

- **Obtain Authorization** – Never scan or test systems without explicit permission from the owner.
- **Follow Responsible Disclosure Policies** – If you find a vulnerability, report it responsibly instead of exploiting it.
- **Do No Harm** – Avoid actions that could damage, disrupt, or compromise the integrity of systems and networks.
- **Respect Privacy** – Do not access, store, or share sensitive data without proper authorization.
- **Stay Transparent** – Keep clear records of your actions and communicate openly with stakeholders.
- **Comply with Legal Frameworks** – Always ensure your activities align with the laws and regulations of your jurisdiction.

Responsible Disclosure and Reporting Vulnerabilities

Discovering a security vulnerability is only part of the ethical hacking process. How you handle and report it is equally important. Follow these steps for responsible disclosure:

1. **Confirm the Vulnerability** – Ensure that the issue is legitimate and reproducible.
2. **Identify the Right Contact** – Locate the responsible security team or designated disclosure program (e.g., a bug bounty platform).
3. **Report Privately** – Do not publicly disclose the vulnerability before notifying the affected party.
4. **Provide Clear Details** – Include steps to reproduce the issue, potential risks, and possible fixes.
5. **Allow Time for Remediation** – Give the organization time to address the issue before making it public.
6. **Follow Up Respectfully** – If there is no response, consider escalating through appropriate channels, such as CERT (Computer Emergency Response Teams).

Many organizations have responsible disclosure policies or bug bounty programs where ethical hackers can report vulnerabilities and receive recognition or rewards.

Understanding Laws Related to Cybersecurity Research

Cybersecurity research and ethical hacking exist in a legal gray area in some jurisdictions. Before using Shodan or conducting security assessments, it's important to understand the relevant laws, including:

Computer Fraud and Abuse Act (CFAA) - USA

The CFAA criminalizes unauthorized access to computer systems. Even scanning without explicit permission could lead to legal consequences.

General Data Protection Regulation (GDPR) - EU

GDPR imposes strict rules on handling personal data. Unauthorized collection or storage of exposed data through Shodan searches could violate privacy laws.

Cybercrime Laws by Country

Each country has specific cybercrime laws regulating unauthorized access, hacking, and data breaches. Examples include:

- **UK:** Computer Misuse Act
- **Canada:** Criminal Code (Section 342.1 - Unauthorized Use of a Computer)
- **Australia:** Cybercrime Act 2001

Bug Bounty and Disclosure Programs

Many companies and governments have formal vulnerability disclosure programs (VDPs) that provide a legal avenue for reporting security issues. Always check if an organization has a VDP before reporting a vulnerability.

Best Practices for Legal Compliance

- **Read Terms of Service** – Understand the rules of platforms like Shodan before conducting research.
- **Use Honeypots and Test Environments** – Perform research on controlled systems instead of real-world targets.
- **Seek Legal Advice** – If unsure, consult a cybersecurity lawyer before engaging in security research.
- **Document Your Actions** – Keep logs of your activities to prove good intent and compliance.

Conclusion

Using Shodan responsibly requires adherence to ethical hacking principles, responsible disclosure processes, and an understanding of legal frameworks. Always ensure you have proper authorization, follow best practices, and stay informed about the latest cybersecurity laws to avoid unintended legal consequences. Ethical hacking, when done correctly, can contribute to a safer and more secure digital world.

Chapter 10: Conclusion & Future of Shodan

Shodan has revolutionized **cybersecurity, ethical hacking, and Open-Source Intelligence (OSINT)** by providing a unique way to **scan and analyze internet-connected devices**. As cyber threats continue to evolve, so does Shodan, adapting with **AI-driven automation, deeper network insights, and integration with other security tools**.

In this final chapter, we will explore:

- **How Shodan is evolving with AI and automation**
- **Other cybersecurity tools that complement Shodan**
- **Next steps: OSINT, penetration testing, and ethical hacking certifications**

---

1. How Shodan is Evolving with AI and Automation

Shodan is continuously improving its capabilities, particularly by leveraging **AI and automation** to:

AI-Powered Threat Detection

- **Machine learning algorithms** can analyze Shodan's vast dataset to **identify abnormal patterns**, such as:
  - A sudden spike in **exposed databases**
  - Newly infected IoT botnets
  - Emerging **zero-day vulnerabilities** being exploited
- **AI-powered anomaly detection** helps cybersecurity teams act **before** a breach happens.

Automated Network Monitoring & Alerts

- Organizations can now **automate Shodan searches** to **receive alerts** when their network has:
  - **New open ports**
  - **Exposed devices**
  - **Misconfigured services**
- **Integration with SIEM (Security Information and Event Management) tools** allows security teams to **track Shodan data in real-time**.

Deeper OSINT & Cyber Intelligence

- Shodan is increasingly being used for **real-time intelligence gathering** to detect:
  - **Nation-state cyber operations**
  - **Critical infrastructure vulnerabilities**
  - **Cybercriminal activities on underground forums**

As Shodan expands its **AI and automation capabilities**, it will become even more essential for **defensive and offensive cybersecurity operations**.

2. Other Cybersecurity Tools That Complement Shodan

While Shodan is **a powerful tool for discovering internet-exposed devices**, it works best when **combined with other cybersecurity tools**.

Tool	Purpose
Censys	Similar to Shodan, but provides more **detailed certificate analysis** for tracking hosts.
Google Dorking	Uses **Google search operators** to find **exposed files, login portals, and misconfigured sites**.
Nmap	A **network scanning tool** to map **open ports, services, and vulnerabilities**.
Metasploit	A penetration testing framework for **exploiting security weaknesses**.
Maltego	Used for **OSINT investigations** and mapping **threat actors**.
Wireshark	Captures and analyzes **network traffic** for security audits.

Each of these tools enhances **Shodan's capabilities** by providing **deeper analysis, penetration testing options, and OSINT intelligence**.

3. Next Steps: OSINT, Penetration Testing, and Ethical Hacking Certifications

Now that you have **mastered Shodan**, where should you go next? Here are some **practical next steps** to **level up your cybersecurity skills**:

OSINT (Open-Source Intelligence)

- Learn how to **collect intelligence** using public sources like:
  - **Shodan, Censys, Maltego, HaveIBeenPwned**
  - **Google Dorking & social media monitoring tools**
- Consider taking an **OSINT certification**, such as:
  - **Certified OSINT Professional (COP)**
  - **SANS SEC487: OSINT Gathering & Analysis**

Penetration Testing & Ethical Hacking

- Expand your skills by **learning penetration testing frameworks** like:
  - **Metasploit** (for exploitation)
  - **Burp Suite** (for web application testing)
  - **Kali Linux tools** (for network and system testing)
- Get **certified** to validate your expertise:
  - **Certified Ethical Hacker (CEH)**

- o **Offensive Security Certified Professional (OSCP)**
- o **GIAC Penetration Tester (GPEN)**

Cybersecurity Career Pathways

Shodan is widely used by:

- **Cybersecurity analysts** (to monitor corporate networks)
- **Penetration testers** (to find vulnerabilities)
- **Threat intelligence researchers** (to track cybercriminal activities)
- **Government agencies** (to secure critical infrastructure)

If you want to build a **career in cybersecurity**, mastering **Shodan and OSINT tools** is a **great starting point**.

Final Thoughts

Shodan is more than just a **search engine for the internet**—it is a **critical cybersecurity tool** that can:

- ✓ **Detect exposed devices and misconfigurations**
- ✓ **Assist ethical hackers in penetration testing**
- ✓ **Help businesses secure their networks**
- ✓ **Provide OSINT intelligence for cyber defense**

As cybersecurity threats continue to evolve, **Shodan will remain a powerful ally** in **staying ahead of attackers**.

Table Of Contents